# PLAYTIME

## Englisch für Kinder

Band 1

von

Hannelore Gottschalk

TR-Verlagsunion

Die Sendereihe PLAYTIME ist eine Produktion des Bayerischen Rundfunks / Redaktion Sprachen.
Autorin: Hannelore Gottschalk; Mitarbeit: Ines Baumer-Huber, Leonora Fröhlich-Ward;
Fachdidaktische Beratung: Hanns Höfer;
Regie: Raimund M. Maxsein;
Moderation der Sendereihe: Helen Lanzer.

4. unveränderte Auflage 1990

Fotos und Umschlaggestaltung: Raimund M. Maxsein, München
Zeichnungen: Linda-Film, Curt Linda, München
Layout der Comics: Wolfgang Dietrich, München
Layout der Bilderrätsel: Erica Heisinger, München
Noten im Buch: Heinz Loch, München
Gesamtherstellung: Druckerei Bremberger, München
ISBN: 3-8058-1963-3

Liebe Kinder,

dieses PLAYTIME-Buch enthält alles, was ihr aus der Fernsehsendung kennt: Bilder von unseren Trickfiguren Jack und Jill, die lustigen Zeichnungen zu den Geschichten, die Lieder und Reime. Die illustrierten PLAYTIME-Wörter und die Geschichten könnt ihr selbst ausmalen, die Lieder mitsingen oder auf einem Instrument nachspielen.

Damit es euch nicht langweilig wird, könnt ihr auch einige Bilderrätsel lösen oder wie zum Beispiel auf Seite 15 "Snakes and Ladders" spielen. Bei diesem Schlangen- und Leiterspiel wird reihum gewürfelt. Wer auf eine Schlange gerät, muß herunter – you go down the snake –, wer an eine Leiter kommt, darf hinaufsteigen – you go up the ladder. Gewonnen hat, wer als erster genau ins Ziel kommt.

Ihr werdet sehen, wie spannend es ist, eine fremde Sprache verstehen zu lernen, vor allem, weil ihr doch alle freiwillig mitmacht. Vielleicht begegnet ihr auch einmal Kindern aus England, aus Amerika oder aus einem anderen englischsprachigen Land. Da werdet ihr dann sehen, wie schnell ihr Kontakt habt.

Viel Spaß also mit PLAYTIME!

* * *

Liebe Eltern,

PLAYTIME ist eine Sendereihe, die Kinder ab etwa fünf Jahren in einen ersten Kontakt mit der englischen Sprache bringen will. Und dies auf spielerische Weise, durch eine Folge von heiter aufgebauten Szenen mit Trickfiguren, durch Lieder und Ratespiele, die – wie wir während unserer Produktion bereits testen konnten – den Kindern Freude machen. Wir haben uns bemüht, alle Geschichten so einprägsam aufzubauen, daß sie vom Hören und Verstehen zum kreativen und spielerischen Umgang mit der fremden Sprache führen.

Auch wenn die ganz Kleinen dieses Buch noch nicht lesen können, bei PLAYTIME finden sie genug Anregungen zum Mitmachen. Unsere englische Moderatorin fordert in den Sendungen immer wieder zum Nachsprechen oder auch zum Mitsingen auf. Dadurch werden Gehör und Ausdruck frühzeitig geschult, und die Kinder unmerklich zu einer korrekten Aussprache angeleitet.

Sicher wird sich auch Ihr Kind auf diese Weise in einer zunehmend mehrsprachigen Welt leichter zurechtfinden, nicht nur in der später weiterführenden Schule.

Vielleicht macht es Ihnen selbst Spaß, zusammen mit Ihrem Kind bei PLAYTIME mitzumachen? Es würde sich bestimmt darüber freuen, so wie auch wir von PLAYTIME.

Hannelore Gottschalk

INHALTSVERZEICHNIS

Hello, everybody.
My name's Helen.

Welcome to
PLAYTIME
and
welcome to
this book!

Hello, children.
My name's Jill.

Hi, children.
My name's Jack.

*Hier kannst du*
*dein Bild einkleben.*

What's your name?

My name's

# PLAYTIME WORDS

## Come and speak with us.

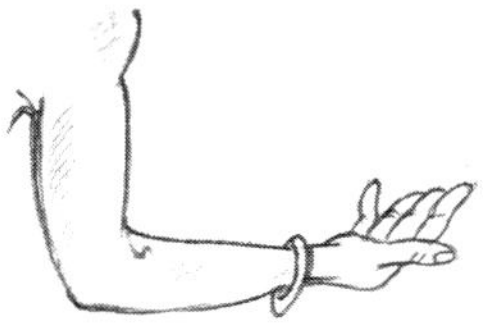

arm

ball

bear

book

doll

hanky

lephant

jelly-bear

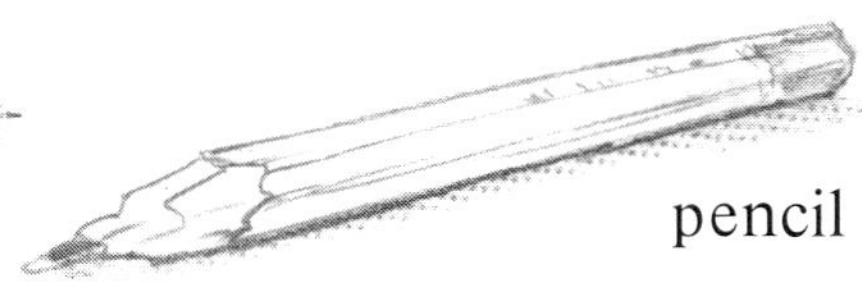

pencil

toybox

## What's in the toybox?

There's a dool
a bear
an elepfant
a ball

Which toy do you want?

I want the . . . . . . . . . . , please.
Thank you.

## Come and count with us.

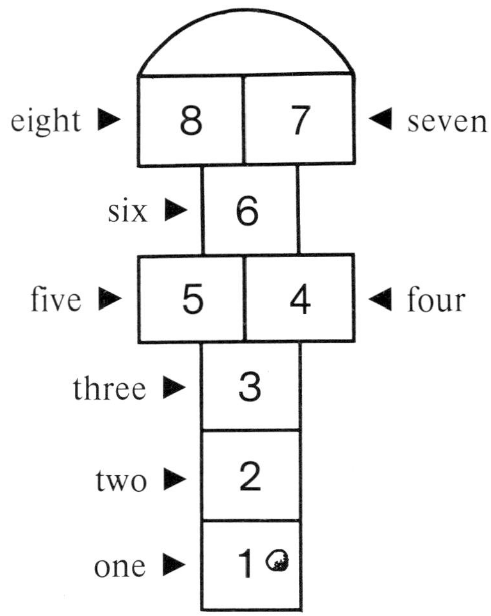

**Come and read with us.**

I can help you Pooh.
Do you want a jelly-bear ?
I want two jelly-bears, please.
Thank you.
Come on, let's play.
Here. Catch !

# Come and sing a song with us.

Music: Rolf Wilhelm
Words: Leonora Fröhlich-Ward, Hannelore Gottschalk

# PICTURE PUZZLE

What's his name?

His name's Pooh

*Wenn du die englischen Namen für die abgebildeten Gegenstände in die Kästchen schreibst und die Buchstaben in den umrandeten Feldern von oben nach unten liest, hast du die Lösung.*

## *Das kannst du jetzt schon:*

| | |
|---|---|
| Hello. | *Hallo. Guten Tag.* |
| My name's . . . | *Ich heiße . . .* |
| What's your name? | *Wie heißt du?* |
| Come and play with me. | *Komm, spiel mit mir.* |
| I want two jelly-bears, please. | *Ich möchte bitte zwei Gummibärchen haben.* |
| Thank you. | *Danke.* |

Lösungen

S. 7 There's a doll, a bear, an elephant, a ball.

S. 11 pencil – doll – book – hanky
His name's Pooh.

Good morning, children.
It's raining today.

Let's play a game.
Let's play snakes and ladders.

You go up the ladder and
down the snake.

Here are the counters:
red yellow blue green

Which counter do you want?
I want the ...green... counter,
please.

# PLAYTIME WORDS

## Come and speak with us.

mouse

ladder

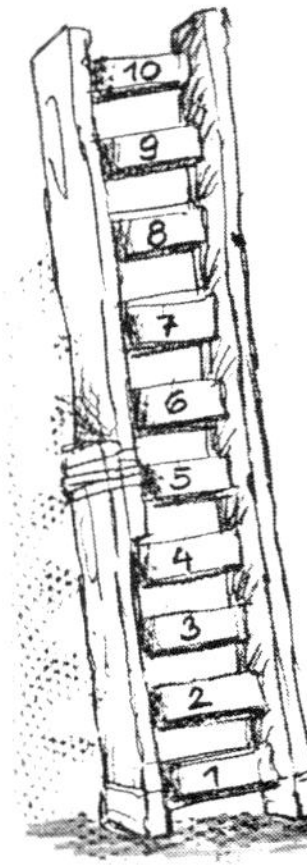

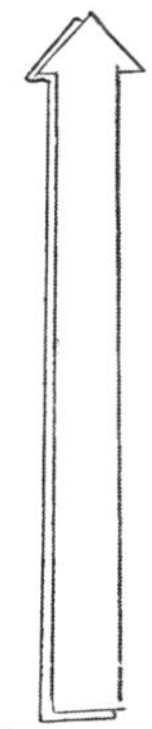

up

snake

down

raincoat

boots

rain

umbrella

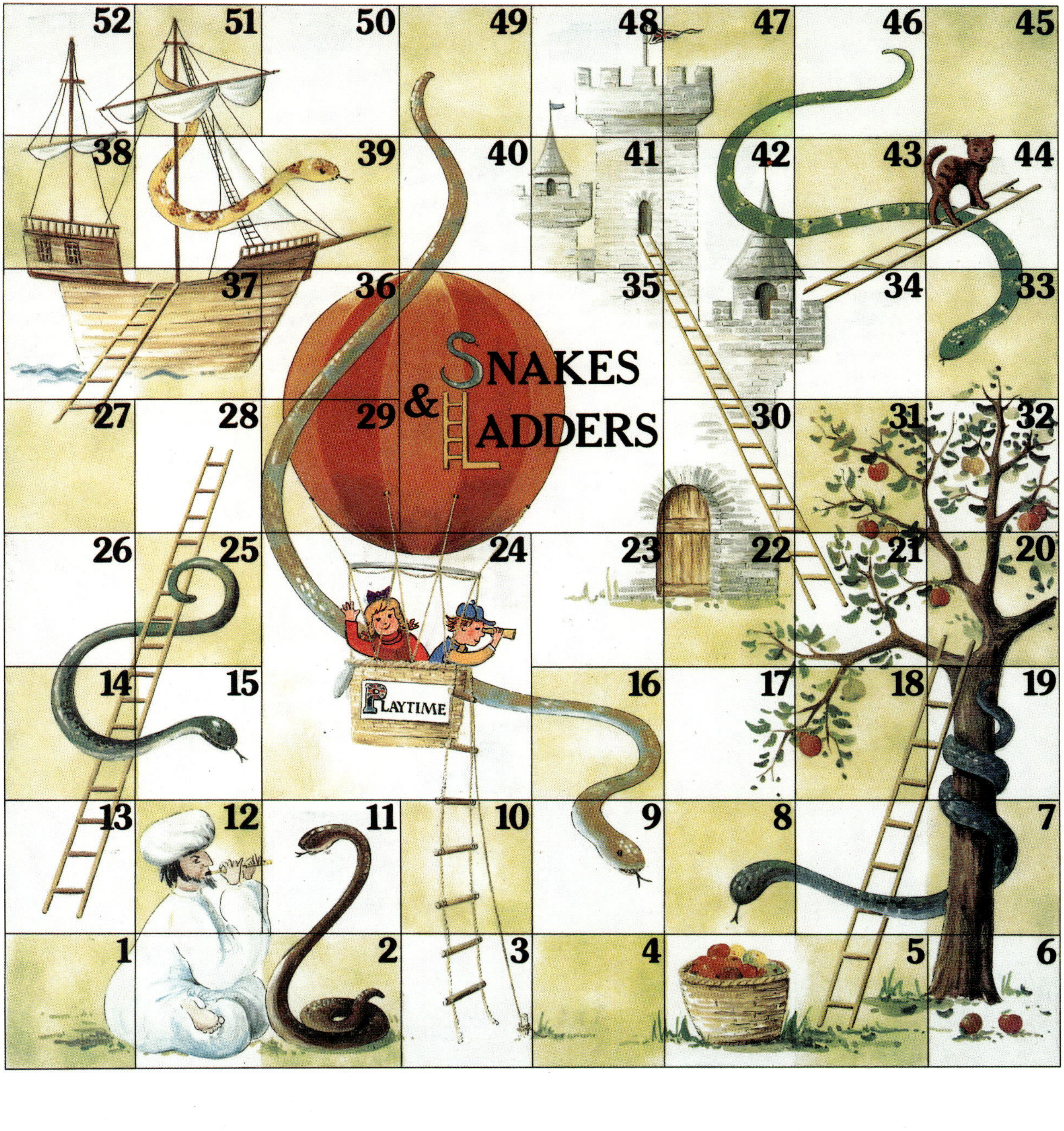

SNAKES & LADDERS
PLAYTIME
52
51
50
49
48
47
46
45
38
39
40
41
42
43
44
37
36
35
34
33
27
28
29
30
31
32
26
25
24
23
22
21
20
14
15
16
17
18
19
13
12
11
10
9
8
7
1
2
3
4
5
6

**Come and read with us.**

I'm the winner.
I'm the winner.
It's a silly game.
I don't like snakes and ladders.
Come on, Jill.
Let's go outside.
All right.
Where's my raincoat ?
Here it is. Put it on.
Here are your boots and here's your umbrella.
I can't get the boot on.
There's something inside.

*Was war in Jills Stiefel?*

| | |
|---|---|
| ☐ | a snake |
| ☒ | a mouse |
| ☐ | a ladder |

*Zähle auf Englisch von 1 bis 10 und verbinde die Zahlen miteinander, dann kannst du die Lösung erkennen.*

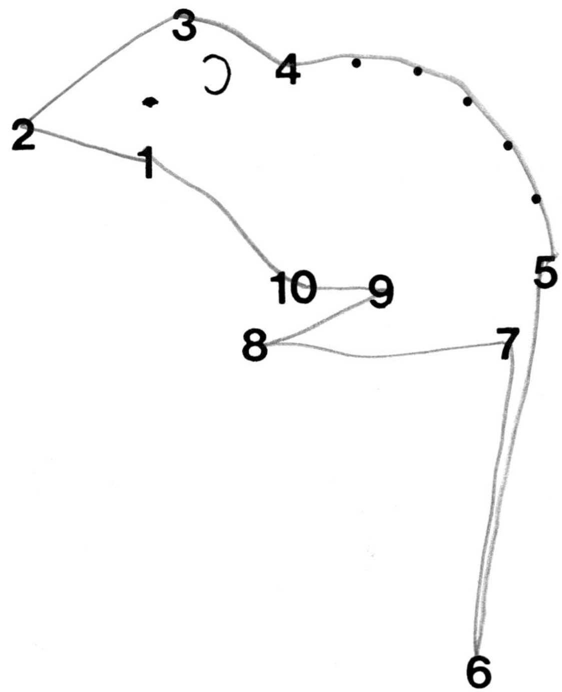

# Come and sing a song with us.

Music: Traditional, adapted by Rolf Wilhelm
Words: Traditional

## PICTURE PUZZLE

It's raining.
Don't forget your . . . . . . . . !

*Das Lösungswort ergibt sich, wenn du die englischen Namen für die Abbildungen in die Kästchen schreibst und die Buchstaben in den umrandeten Feldern von oben nach unten liest.*

## *Das hast du neu dazugelernt:*

| | |
|---|---|
| Good morning. | *Guten Morgen.* |
| Let's play. | *Spielen wir.* |
| Come on, let's finish the game. | *Komm, beenden wir das Spiel.* |
| It's my turn. | *Ich bin an der Reihe.* |
| It's your turn. | *Du bist an der Reihe.* |
| Don't cheat. | *Nicht mogeln.* |
| I'm the winner. | *Ich bin die Siegerin.*<br>*Ich habe gewonnen.* |

Lösungen

S. 18 a mouse
S. 20 1 mouse 2 arm 3 boots 4 raincoat 5 bear 6 ladder 7 ball 8 snake
Don't forget your umbrella!

Let's go to the fair.

Look at the roundabout.
Which animal do you want to ride on?

I want to ride on the

- [ ] swan
- [ ] horse
- [ ] giraffe
- [x] bear

# PLAYTIME WORDS

## Come and speak with us.

monkey

swan

horse

animals

giraffe

roundabout

token

orange juice

car

hamburger

**Come and read with us.**

Pull, Jack, pull.
It's a doll.
I don't want the doll.
Now it's my turn.
It's the car.
I like the car.
Give me the car, please.
You can have the doll.
No. It's my car.
I don't want the doll.

**Look at the picture.**

You can't win a . . . . . . . . . . here.

- [ ] doll
- [ ] car
- [x] hamburger
- [x] snake
- [ ] ball

**Jack has got a present for Helen.**

What is it?

It's a snake

## Come and sing a song with us.

Music: Traditional, adapted by Rolf Wilhelm
Words: Henry J. Sayers

Where's Pooh?

Pooh is on the roundabout.

# PICTURE PUZZLE

*Weißt du, wie diese Tiere auf englisch heißen? Wenn du die englischen Namen in die Kästchen schreibst und die umrandeten Felder von oben nach unten liest, hast du das englische Wort für „Tiere“.*

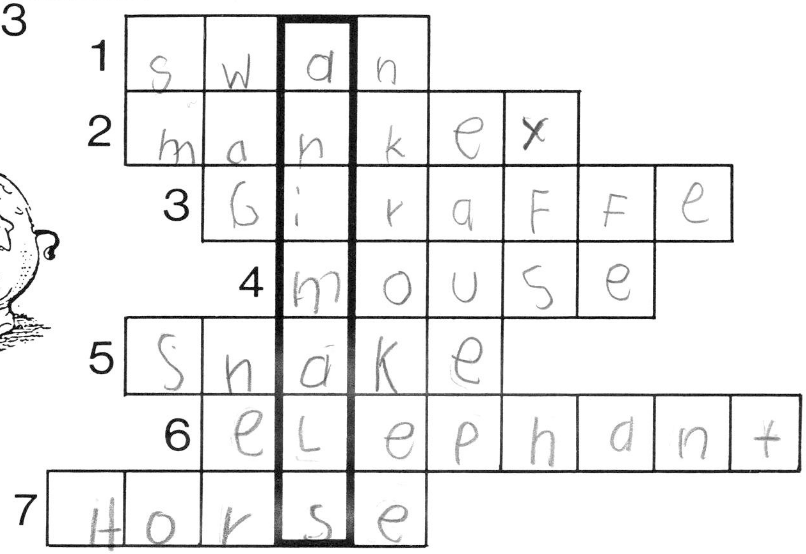

## *Das hast du neu dazugelernt:*

| | |
|---|---|
| Good afternoon! | *Guten Tag. (Begrüßung am Nachmittag.)* |
| I'm hungry. | *Ich habe Hunger.* |
| I'm thirsty. | *Ich habe Durst.* |
| I like hamburgers. | *Ich mag Hamburger. Ich esse gerne Hamburger.* |
| I like orange juice. | *Ich mag Orangensaft. Ich trinke gerne Orangensaft.* |
| Give me the car, please. | *Gib mir bitte das Auto.* |
| I don't want the doll. | *Ich möchte die Puppe nicht haben.* |
| Where's Pooh? | *Wo ist Pooh?* |

Lösungen

S. 26 hamburger
It's a snake.
S. 27 roundabout
S. 28 1 swan 2 monkey 3 giraffe 4 mouse 5 snake 6 elephant 7 horse
animals

What are you doing, Jack?

I'm painting.

Come on, children,
paint your
dream house.

# PLAYTIME WORDS

## Come and speak with us.

## Come and read with us.

What a funny house !
Is this your dream house ?
Yes - here's the roof
and this is the chimney.
What's this ?
It's a flower.
My picture's finished.

## Come and sing a song with us.

Music: Rolf Wilhelm
Words: Traditional, adapted by Leonora Fröhlich-Ward

Ding, dong, dot Pooh is in the pot Look at him in there Poor Pooh the bear!

Ding, dong, dine
Pooh is on the line
Look at him up there
Poor Pooh the bear!

Ding, dong, dar
Pooh is in the car
Look at him in there
Pooh is a funny bear!

Tell me where Pooh is.
Look at the pictures
on page 34.

1 Pooh is in the not

2 Pooh is on the eine

3 Pooh is in the car

**Where's Jack's brush?**

It's under the chair

*Das hast du neu dazugelernt:*

| | |
|---|---|
| What are you doing? | *Was machst du gerade?* |
| I'm painting a house. | *Ich male ein Haus.* |
| Careful. Don't touch. | *Vorsicht! Nicht berühren!* |
| Where's my brush? | *Wo ist mein Pinsel?* |
| It's under the chair. | *Er liegt unter dem Stuhl.* |
| My picture's finished. | *Mein Bild ist fertig.* |

Lösungen

1 in the pot 2 on the line 3 in the car
It's under the chair.

**Here's Pooh's house.**

*Kannst du diese Wörter in der richtigen Reihenfolge unter die Pfeile schreiben?*

window
roof
door
chimney
flowers

*Kannst du Pooh beim Beschriften der Farbtöpfe helfen?*

red
brown
green

blue
orange
yellow

# UNIT FIVE JILL'S BIRTHDAY 5

Happy birthday, Jill.
Look – I've got a present for you.

Thank you, Jack.
I'm six today.
My birthday is in April.

How old are you?

I'm eight8

When's your birthday?

My birthday is in November 17.91

# PLAYTIME WORDS

## Come and speak with us.

## Come and sing a song with us.

Music and words: Traditional

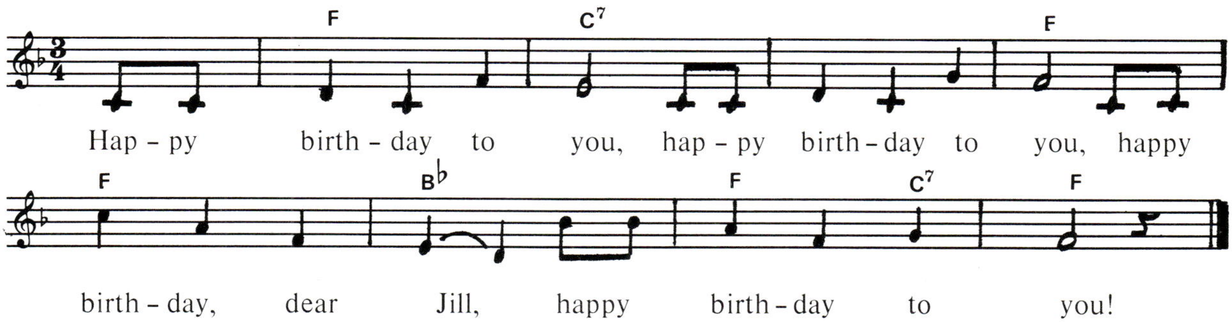

## Come and read with us.

What's that, Jill ?
It's my magic box.
It's a present from Helen.
This is my magic key.
Turn the key, turn the key,
Turn the key around,
Turn the key,
Open the box and listen to the sound.
What a funny birthday party !

**Come and play with us.**

Is Tom a dog?

No, he's elephant . . .

Is Harry a cat?

No, he's dog .

Is Diana an elephant?

No, she's mouse .

Is Lucy a mouse?

No, she's cat .

## Come and sing a song with us.

Music: Rolf Wilhelm
Words: Traditional adapted

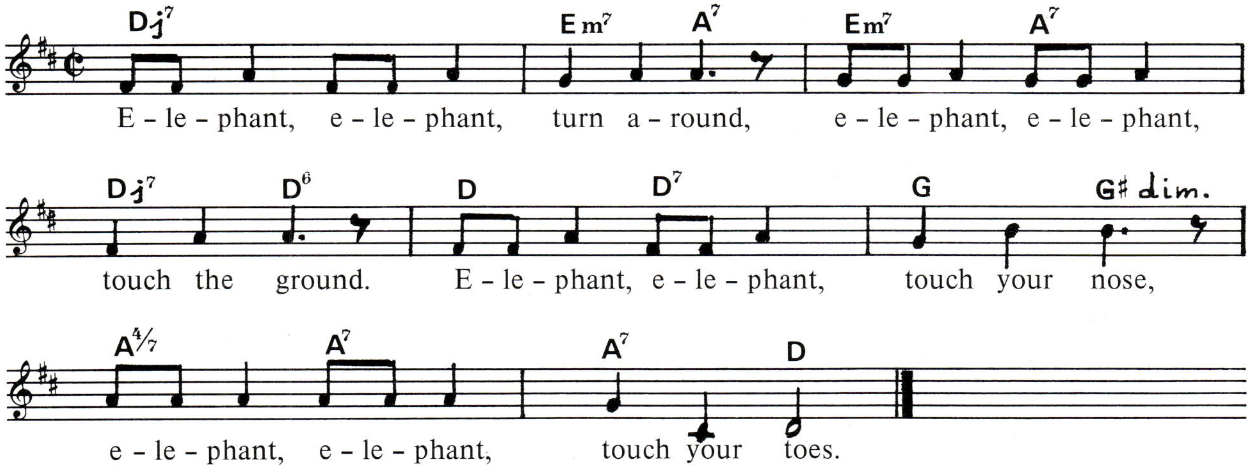


## Colour the balloons.

1 green
2 red
3 blue
4 yellow
5 brown
6 orange

**How old is Jill today?**

She's six today.

**What's missing from the magic box?**

*Wenn du die Namen der gezeichneten Gegenstände in die Kästchen schreibst und die umrandeten Felder von oben nach unten liest, hast du das Lösungswort.*

1 Have some 

2 Pooh has got a 

for Helen.

3 He's playing the 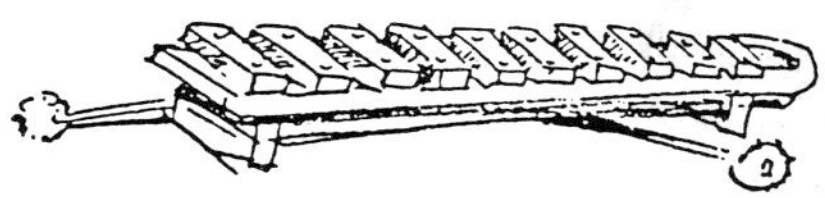

| | | | | | | | | | |
|---|---|---|---|---|---|---|---|---|---|
| 1 | c | a | k | e | | | | | |
| 2 | | L | e | t | t | e | r | | |
| 3 | | x | y | L | o | p | h | o | n | e |

*Das hast du neu dazugelernt:*

| | |
|---|---|
| Happy birthday, Jill! | *Alles Gute zum Geburtstag, Jill!* |
| How old are you? | *Wie alt bist du?* |
| I'm six. | *Ich bin sechs.* |
| When's your birthday? | *Wann ist dein Geburtstag?* |
| My birthday is in . . . . | *Mein Geburtstag ist im . . . .* |
| Have some cake! | *Nimm dir Kuchen!* |

What's her name?

Lösungen

S. 42 No, he's an elephant. No, he's a dog. No, she's a mouse. No, she's a cat.
S. 44 She's six today.
1 cake 2 letter 3 xylophone
key

# A BIKE TOUR

Come on, Jill.
Let's go on a bike tour.

That's a good idea.

I can't ride.
My legs are too short.

Have you got a bike?

| | |
|---|---|
| X | Yes, I have. |
| | No, I haven't. |

# PLAYTIME WORDS

## Come and speak with us.

apple

banana

sun

biscuit

basket

blanket

tree

bike

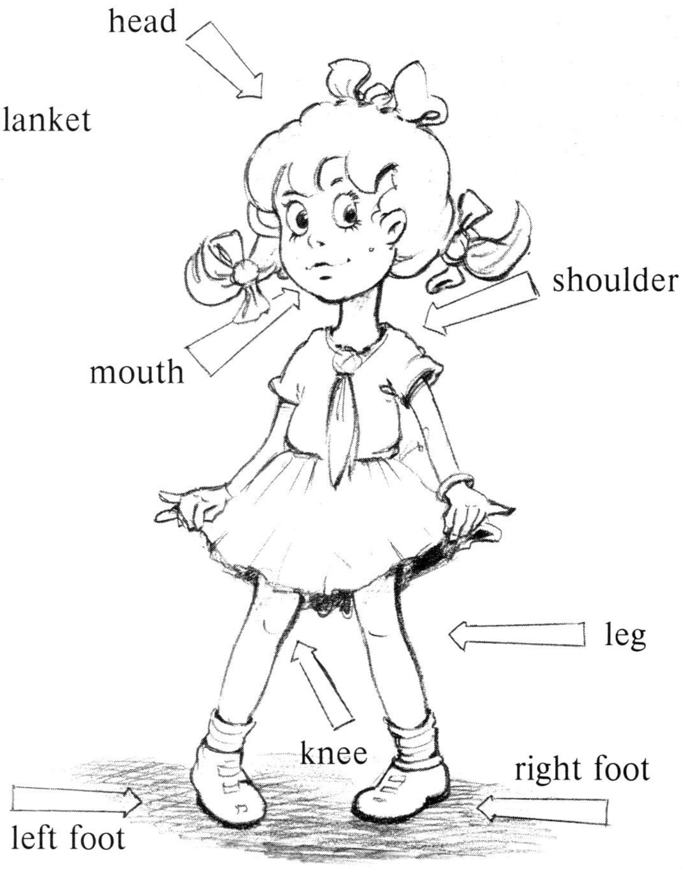

**Come and read with us.**

Poor Jack !
Are you hungry ?
Yes, I am.
Have you got a banana ?
No, I haven't.
Have an apple !
Thank you.

## Come and sing a song with us.

Music: Traditional, adapted by Rolf Wilhelm
Words: Traditional, adapted by Ines Baumer-Huber

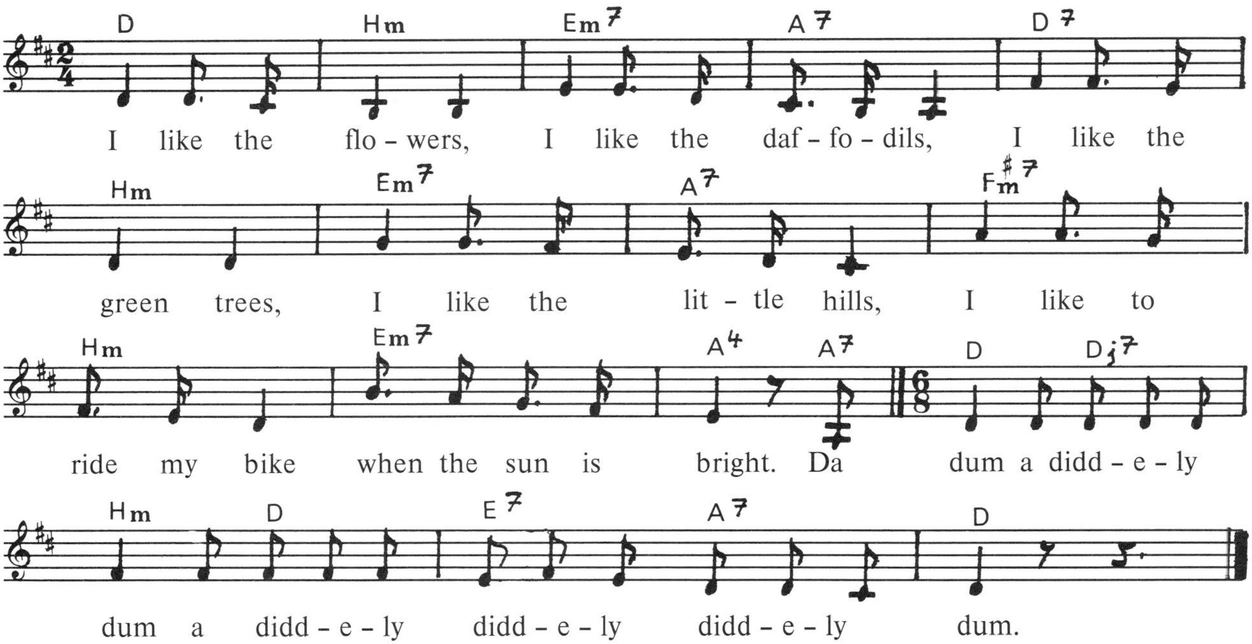

## Come and sing a song with us.

Music: Traditional, adapted by Rolf Wilhelm
Words: Traditional

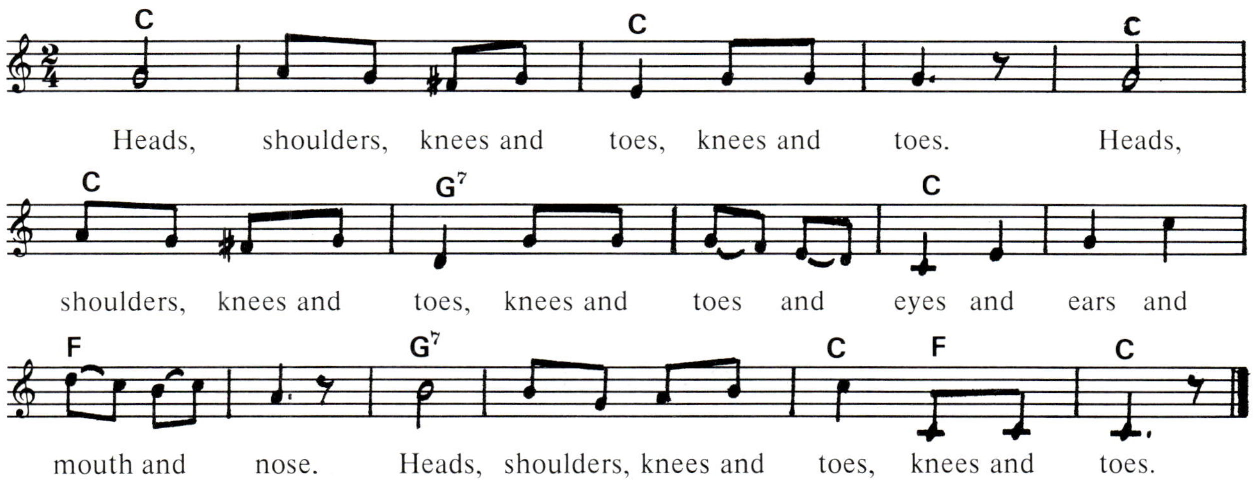

# PICTURE PUZZLE

Pooh is hungry.

What's he doing?

He's eating a banana.

*Wenn du die englischen Namen für die Abbildungen der Reihe nach in die Kästchen schreibst und die umrandeten Felder von oben nach unten liest, hast du die gesuchte Tätigkeit.*

1

2

3

4

5

| | | | | | | | | | | |
|---|---|---|---|---|---|---|---|---|---|---|
| | | 1 | b | i | k | e | | | | |
| | | | | 2 | b | a | s | k | e | t |
| | | | | | 3 | T | r | e | e | |
| 4 | b | i | s | c | u | i | t | | | |
| | 5 | b | a | n | a | n | a | | | |
| | | | 6 | L | e | g | | | | |

6

## *Das hast du neu dazugelernt:*

| | |
|---|---|
| Have you got a banana?<br>No, I haven't. | *Hast du eine Banane?*<br>*Nein.* |
| Are you hungry?<br>Yes, I am. | *Hast du Hunger?*<br>*Ja.* |
| Are you ready?<br>No, I'm not. | *Bist du fertig?*<br>*Nein.* |
| Hurry up! | *Beeil dich!* |
| Watch out! | *Vorsicht! Paß auf!* |
| Don't cry! | *Weine nicht!* |
| That's a good idea! | *Das ist eine gute Idee!* |

Lösungen

S. 52 1 bike 2 basket 3 tree 4 biscuit 5 banana 6 leg
He's eating a banana.

Hello, children.
Welcome to the toy museum.

I like dolls.

I don't like the rocking-horse.

## PLAYTIME WORDS

### Come and speak with us.

a doll's house

bedroom

bathroom

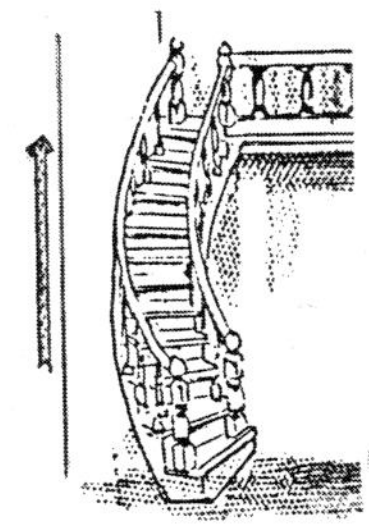

upstairs

kitchen

living-room

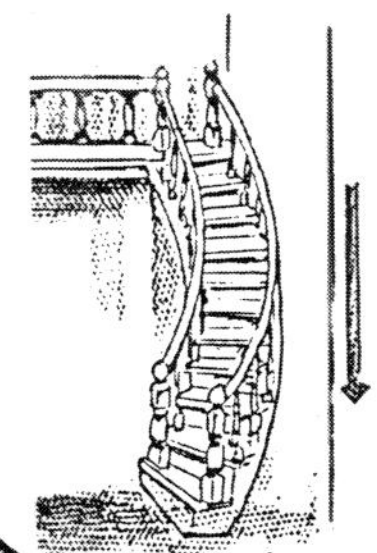

downstairs

rocking-horse

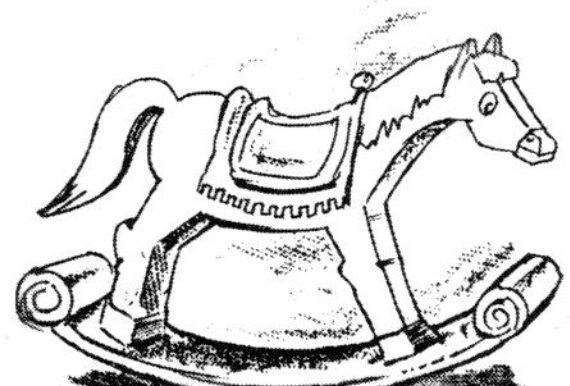

motorbike

drums

(news)paper

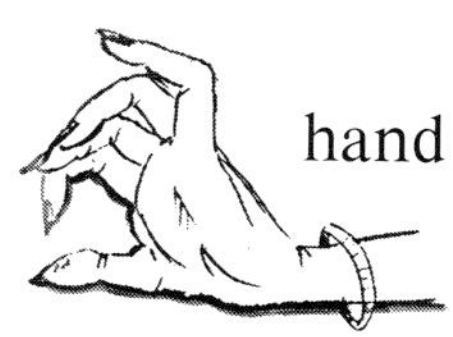

hand

**Come and read with us.**

Father Cat is in the kitchen.
He's making a cake.
Tom is playing the drums in the bedroom.
TOM
There's Grandpa - behind the house.
He's fixing his motorbike.
THE CATS
What a funny family !

**Where are the rooms?**

Upstairs  or 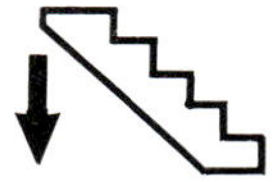 downstairs?

Where's the bedroom? It's Upstairs

Where's the kitchen? It's downstairs

Where's the living-room? It's downstairs

Where's the bathroom? It's upstairs

**What are they doing?**

*Welche Karten gehören zusammen?*

He's making

She's reading

He's playing

She's washing

**What have they got?**

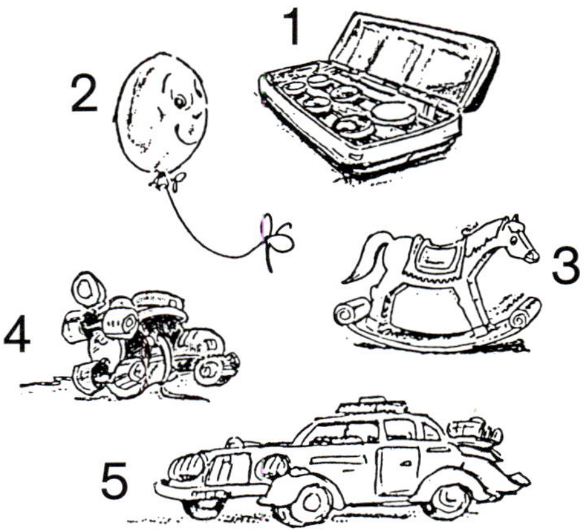


1 He's got a paintbox

2 She's got a ballon

3 He's got a rocking-horse

4 She's got rollerskates

5 He's got a car

**The Cats**

What a funny FAMILY !

*Ein Wort paßt nicht in die Reihe. Suche die falschen Wörter heraus und notiere dir die Anfangsbuchstaben. Sie ergeben das Lösungswort.*

A mouth – nose – eyes – flower
B arm – roof – chimney – door
C bedroom – monkey – kitchen – bathroom
D grandpa – mother – father – I
E drums – piano – letter – xylophone
F snake – mouse – cat – yellow

## Come and sing a song with us.

Music: Rolf Wilhelm
Words: Traditional

## *Das hast du neu dazugelernt:*

| | |
|---|---|
| I like dolls. | *Ich mag Puppen.* |
| I don't like the rocking-horse. | *Ich mag das Schaukelpferd nicht.* |
| She's reading the paper. | *Sie liest Zeitung.* |
| He's making a cake. | *Er macht einen Kuchen.* |
| He's playing the drums. | *Er spielt Trommel.* |
| He's fixing his motorbike. | *Er repariert sein Motorrad.* |
| She's washing her hands. | *Sie wäscht sich die Hände.* |

Lösungen

S. 58 The bedroom is upstairs. The kitchen is downstairs. The living-room is downstairs.
The bathroom is upstairs.

S. 59 She's reading the paper. He's playing the drums. She's washing her hands.
He's making a cake.

S. 60 1 paintbox 2 balloon 3 rocking-horse 4 rollerskates 5 car
A flower B arm C monkey D I E letter F yellow
What a funny family!

What's the time?

It's nine o'clock.

When is the train leaving?

It's leaving at ten o'clock.

# PLAYTIME WORDS

## Come and speak with us.

train

bridge

suitcase

cap

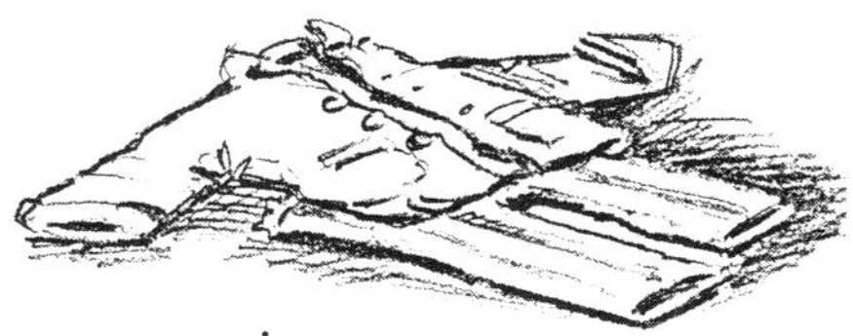

pyjamas

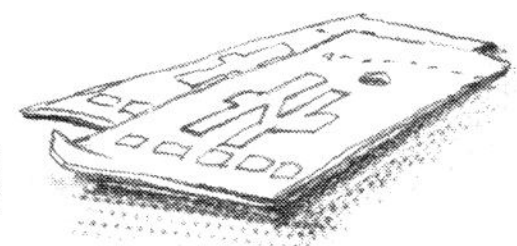

tickets

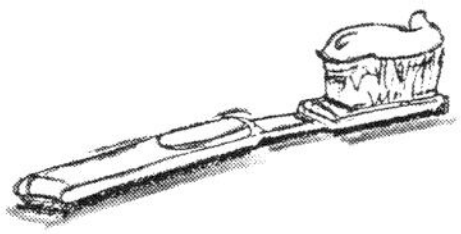

toothbrush

tunnel

boat

castle

It's eleven o'clock

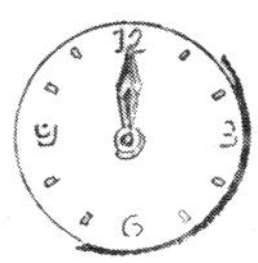

It's twelve o'clock

river

## Come and sing a song with us.

Music: Traditional, adapted by Rolf Wilhelm
Words: Leonora Fröhlich-Ward

### Is it "over", "under" or "on"?

The train is going over a bridge.

There's a river under the bridge.

There are boats on the river.

**What's the time?**

It's twelve o'clock.

It's eight o'clock.

It's seven o'clock.

It's three o'clock.

## *Das hast du neu dazugelernt:*

| | |
|---|---|
| What's the time? | *Wie spät ist es?* |
| It's nine o'clock. | *Es ist neun Uhr.* |
| When is the train leaving? | *Wann geht der Zug?* |
| It's leaving at 10 o'clock. | *Er geht um zehn Uhr.* |
| The train is going over a bridge. | *Der Zug fährt über eine Brücke.* |
| We're going through a tunnel. | *Wir fahren durch einen Tunnel.* |
| Have a good time! | *Schöne Zeit!* |
| Goodbye. | *Auf Wiedersehen.* |

Lösungen

S. 64 over – under – on    S. 65 twelve – eight – seven – three

S. 68 across = waagrecht: book – toothbrush – paintbox – candle

down = senkrecht: tickets – suitcase – boots – umbrella

Scotland

## Come and read with us.

Where are the tickets ?
Here they are, in your cap.
Thank you. Have a good time !
Look Jack, a castle !
A castle ? Where ?
You can't see the castle now. We're going through a tunnel.
There it is. Behind you.
Where's the castle ?

# PICTURE PUZZLE

*Wohin geht die Reise?*

*Die abgebildeten Gegenstände nehmen Jack und Jill auf ihre Reise mit. Löse zuerst das Bilderrätsel. Die Buchstaben in den numerierten Feldern ergeben das Reiseziel.*

# UNIT NINE AT GRANDPA'S 9

Hello, Helen.
How are you?

I'm fine, thank you.
How is your holiday?

Super.
Listen, Helen!
Jack is playing
the bagpipes.

What's your phone number?

My phone number is 894860

## PLAYTIME WORDS

### Come and speak with us.

bagpipes

bed

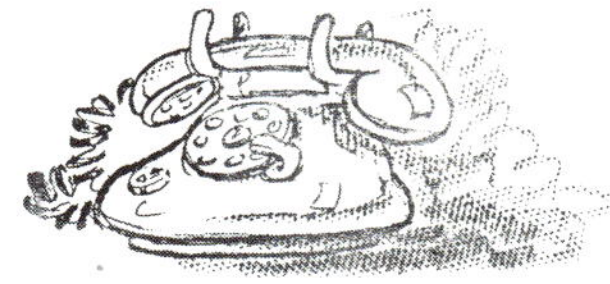

(tele)phone

dress

ghost

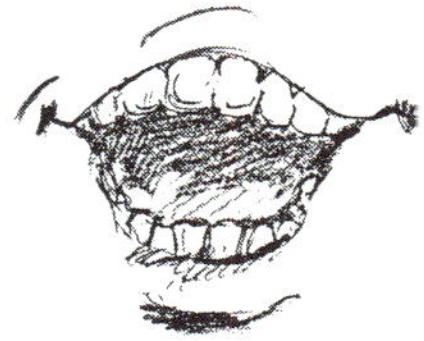

teeth

moon

### Let's play a number game.

Colour the numbers:

green for
eleven-four-two

red for
nine-three-eight

yellow for
seven-ten-six

blue for
twelve-five-one

# Come and sing a song with us.

Music: Rolf Wilhelm
Words: Leonora Fröhlich-Ward, Rolf Wilhelm

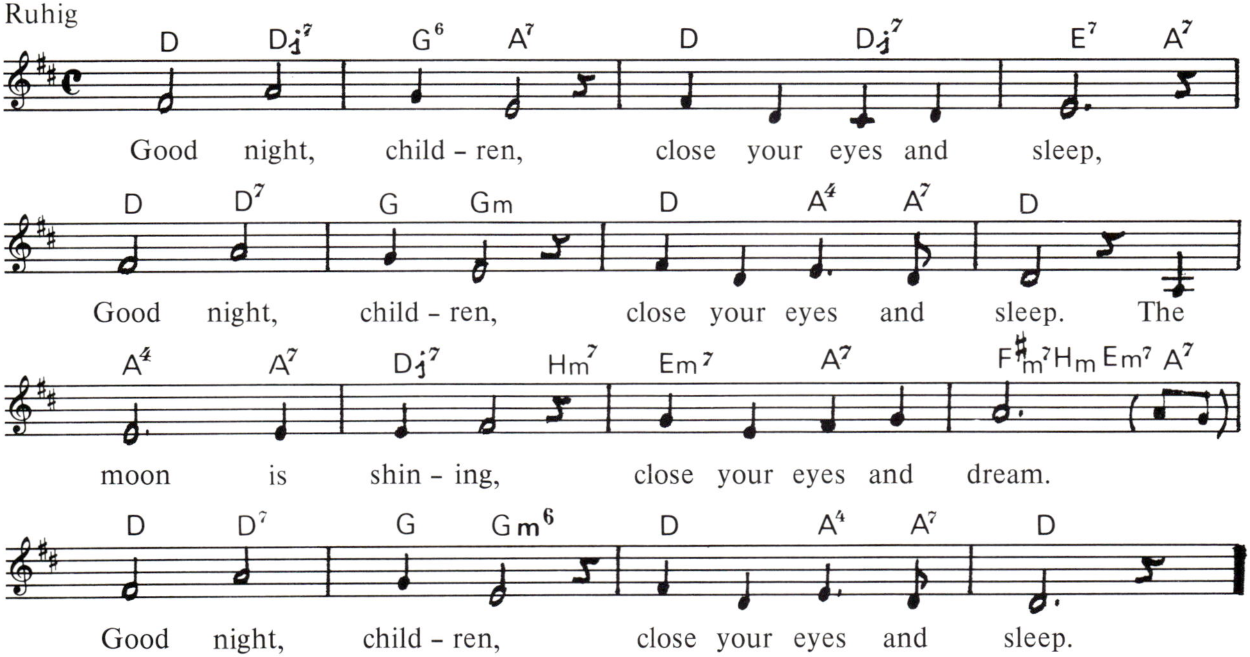

**Come and read with us.**

Don't worry, Jill. There are no ghosts in this house. Good night, children.
Wake up, Jack! Pooh and Penelope are dancing downstairs.
Don't be silly!
Look! Nobody is dancing.

*Welcher Satz gehört zu welchem Bild?*

D What a big apple! A He's awake. C Give me the small brush! B I'm so tired.

A He's awake.

B I'm so tired.

C Give me the small brush!

D What a big apple!

# PUZZLE

In Scotland they play the BAGPIPES.

*Kannst du Nessie beim Auffinden der fehlenden Wörter helfen?*
*Der Endbuchstabe des vorherigen Wortes ist der Anfangsbuchstabe des nächsten Wortes.*
*Die Buchstaben in den umrandeten Feldern ergeben das Lösungswort. Damit es leichter geht, hat Nessie die beiden ersten Wörter schon verraten.*

What is it?

1 You need it for painting.

2 Jack and Jill are hungry. They're eating two . . . . . . . . . . .

3 It's a small animal

4 It's a big animal

5 You need it for your train ride.

6 You put your toys in it.

7 Jack is playing "Happy birthday" on the . . . . . . . . . .

8 You can hear with your . . . .

*Das hast du neu dazugelernt:*

| | |
|---|---|
| What's your phone number? | *Wie ist deine Telefonnummer?* |
| My phone number is . . . . . | *Meine Telefonnummer ist . . . . .* |
| How are you? | *Wie geht es dir?* |
| I'm fine, thank you. | *Danke, mir geht es gut.* |
| I'm tired. | *Ich bin müde.* |
| I'm afraid of ghosts. | *Ich habe Angst vor Gespenstern.* |
| Don't worry! | *Hab' keine Angst!* |
| Good night. | *Gute Nacht.* |

Lösungen

S. *74* A He's awake. B I'm so tired. C Give me the small brush! D What a big apple!
S. *75* brush – hamburgers – snake – elephant – ticket – toybox – xylophone – ears
In Scotland they play the bagpipes.

# UNIT TEN A BOAT RIDE 10

Hello, Helen!
I've got a letter for you.

Dear Helen,

How are you? We're fine. We're going on a boat ride with Grandpa. It's a super holiday.

Love from
Jack and Jill.

What's your address?

My address is . . . . . . .

## PLAYTIME WORDS

### Come and speak with us.

a glass of milk

steering-wheel

lifebelt

cloud

water

ship

helicopter

fog

Nebel

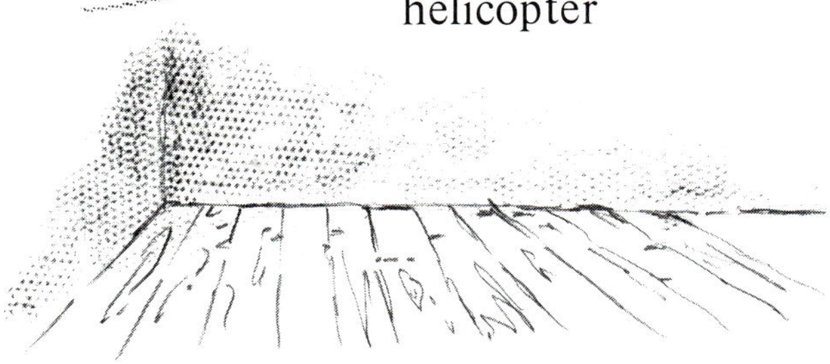

floor

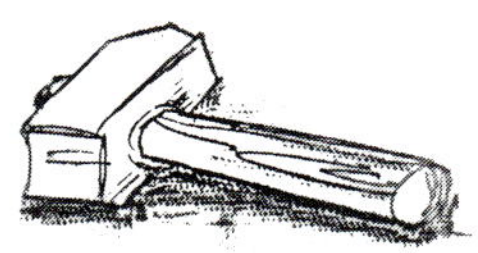

hammer

nail

## Come and sing a song with us.

Music and words: Traditional

## Come and read with us.

We're passing a big ship on our right.
Don't be afraid, Jill.
Look at the clouds.
Look! There's something in the water.
HELP
Quick, throw the lifebelt out.
Pull, Jack, pull!
Hello. My name's Nessie. Thank you.

*Kannst du die Bildunterschriften richtig ergänzen?*

They're playing a game.

They're dancing in the living-room.

They're singing a song.

He's painting a picture.

She's riding her bike.

He's reading a book.

Here are the missing words: singing, painting, reading, playing, riding, dancing

# CROSSWORD PUZZLE

ACROSS

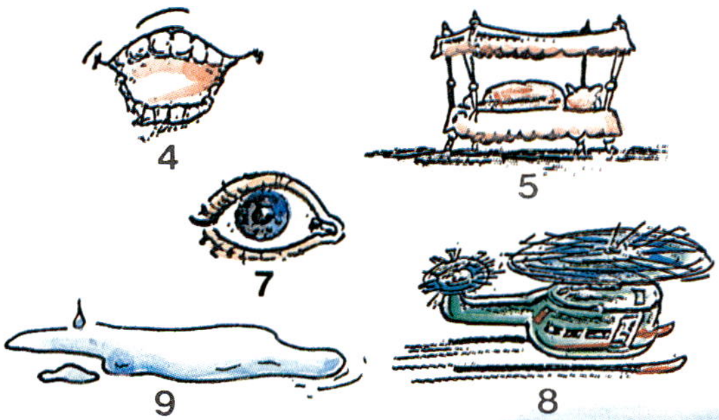


DOWN

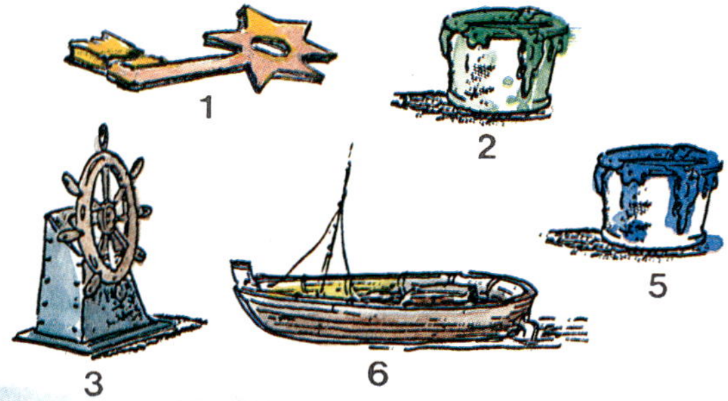

*Das hast du neu dazugelernt:*

| | |
|---|---|
| What's your address? | *Wo wohnst du?* |
| My address is . . . . | *Ich wohne . . . .* |
| Don't be afraid! | *Hab' keine Angst! Fürchte dich nicht!* |
| Oh dear! | *Ach du liebe Zeit!* |
| Sorry. | *Es tut mir leid. Verzeihung!* |
| Turn left. | *Nach links drehen, abbiegen, wenden.* |

Lösungen

S. 82 They're playing a game. He's painting a picture.
They're dancing in the living-room. She's riding her bike.
They're singing a song. He's reading a book.

S. 83 across: teeth – bed – eye – helicopter – water
down: key – green – wheel – blue – boat